GW00385135

We Wear The Crown

by

Lucy Heuschen

First published 2022 by The Hedgehog Poetry Press

Published in the UK by
The Hedgehog Poetry Press
5, Coppack House
Churchill Avenue
Clevedon
BS21 6QW

www.hedgehogpress.co.uk

ISBN: 978-1-913499-97-6

Copyright © Lucy Heuschen 2022

The right of Lucy Heuschen to be identified as the author of this work has been asserted in accordance with the Copyright, Designs and Patents Act 1988.

All rights reserved. No part of this publication may be reproduced, stored in or introduced into a retrieval system, or transmitted in any form, or by any means (electronic, mechanical, photocopying, recording or otherwise) without prior written permissions of the publisher. Any person who does any unauthorised act in relation to this publication may be liable for criminal prosecution and civil claims for damages,

9 8 7 6 5 4 3 2 1

A CIP Catalogue record for this book is available from the British Library.

Cover images by Africa Studio and Jessica Hyde

Images used under license from Shutterstock.com

FOREWORD

In January 2018, I was diagnosed with Stage 2(b) advanced breast cancer.

It was a shock. I had no family history of cancer. I was only 42 years old. I was fairly fit. I was a full-time working lawyer, mother, wife, daughter, sister. But suddenly I was dealing with surgery, chemotherapy, radiotherapy and hormone therapy. In the process, I lost language and gained a new one.

The most challenging part of the process has been finding a path forward after the end of so-called "active treatment". What do you do, after seeing first-hand the fragility of life? My answer was and is, to live better – to do better. To acknowledge and speak my truth. Poetry is a huge part of that.

I hope that these poems shine a light on the impacts of breast cancer during and after treatment – not just for the person who has cancer, but for their loved ones. I'm afraid I have no slick answers to the difficult questions that cancer poses. I can only speak to my own experience.

But I am here to say that there is hope and there are positive life experiences, yes, even after cancer.

*For the two million
newly diagnosed with breast cancer
each year*

*and for my boys, who waited for me
at the top of the steps.*

Contents

THE MOUSE

Soft to the touch, he was given a sweet name
that made him sound normal and reassuring.

What you've found is most likely a breast mouse.
A medieval term. Women have always had them.
Let's book you in for some checks after Christmas.

My mouse endured the crash-bang of panto,
children shrieking *Oh yes he is – oh no he's not.*

Only I could feel him scuttling as mice do,
feel whiskers tickling me, his blood vessels
merging with mine, his body gaining mass.

A touch of fibreglass in place of smooth flesh,
the tail of my breast, the slim tip of a teardrop.

Mouse didn't like light, so I silently apologised
as we went through ultrasound, CT scan, MRI,
a biopsy instrument that penetrated his organs.

It's just like an injection, I have heard. Punch-quick,
nothing to worry about. All quite routine, I said.

At follow-up, we didn't think much of the nurse,
her neutral face. Neither of us knew the meaning
of her presence, the solemn purple of her uniform.

Until we did.

Slow fingers of dusk tapered across the corridor.
My mouse vanished; a dark thing took his place.

REWIND

Unsit the consultant's chair, refeel the simplicity
of a door never opened, unwalk long steps
that echo in a way I don't yet recognise,
unink my name at Reception, forget
that she has seen me cry before,
hush the clandestine doors,

unsee the words, unrip the envelope, shoot it
the wrong way through my letter box
into the hands of a postal worker,
reload their van, crunch gears

invert the great sorting machines, post leaping
like salmon up the rolling ramp to a truck,
its yawning maw ready for breakfast,
fuck with the concept of gravity –

smack my letter down, scrape off the Queen's head,
deface my name and address, unfurl its paper,
iron it ready to receive alternative truth,
dispel the morbidity of black ink,

delete the consultant's name and keep going - DEL
DEL DEL DEL until I reclaim the blank space,
then magnetise the hard drive, wipe out
the last traces of this faithless body.

ADMIRATION

The first time was at 16. I had a plan: how to make
a certain boy jealous. Feigned shop-floor surprise,
Scarlett O'Hara in a cheap polyester uniform.

Oh! Are those for me?

In my twenties, someone else did the honours. Then,
I found out that a single daisy stem can be relied on
to prop up a marriage

for a time. At 36, behind a careworn desk, expecting
an elaborate affair, two dozen costly heads nodding.
All to show the panoramic corner office that here –

here in the closet space was a show worth catching.
Diagnosis at 42 chaos-shuffled the meaning of life
like a post-modern joke. Clockwork blooms arrived.

Honey, another delivery for you.

On and on, at last. All shades except white.

THE TALK

We focus first on identity. Mummy is still your Mummy.
We focus on facts. We love you. We are here for you.
We focus on not saying the unspeakable things.

We pull their small, bony wriggle-bums into our laps.
Only then, we explain that Mummy has to go to hospital.
Careful, so careful not to over-promise.

Then come the questions.

How are you feeling, mummy?
Will the drugs make you feel very sick?
How long before you start feeling better?

Will the doctor put his hand inside you
and pull it out of your boob? Will it hurt?
How much blood do you think there'll be?

It doesn't take long to answer. I'm surprised and relieved.
Like a jab at the doctor's, then finished. I'm OK now;
they're OK. And we hug, hug, hug it out.

WE WEAR THE CROWN

For Ella and Meg

I was warned this stage would come. When my scalp
tingles for the first time, I take my scissors and start.

Each chop aims to conserve my strands, preserve
the maximum. They will form an ebony crown,
to adorn the bare head of a young, sleeping beauty.

I want to share this gift with the princess, with youth
and beauty on her side. I want her to see how much
she can help me – and herself – to keep going.

How she must wake from enforced slumber,
forge new metal. Take my dead cells
and sing them into something new.

Something awake. Something alive.

WE DISCUSS DEMI MOORE IN OUR KITCHEN

You swear
that Demi Moore was always
your ultimate sex symbol.

Ghost-loving, clay-sculpting Demi;
her franchises, car chases, thigh-high,
strip-teasing naughty minx.

Pregnant Demi, a *Vanity Fair* cover girl,
a scandal at the time, hands wrapped
around her eight-month belly.

Demi as a tough military lawyer,
as scarlet-lettered Hester,
as green-eyed Esmerelda,

switching personalities
like award ceremony frocks
to keep a man happy. Failing, failing

but trying again, trying harder:
Demi the ultimate survivalist,
adapting, camouflaging.

I don't know if you mean any or all
of these Demis. We discuss them
over the hum and buzz. Pretend

this is our normal marital debate:
who should have been cast –
who made the best Bond.

As we talk, she asserts herself, struts
through a jungle of dense clippings,
salt-streaked and stubble-cut.

Demi as G.I. Jane.

You say
it suits you.   Think
of Sigourney, Natalie, Charlize.

You say
          I always loved Demi.

WHEN HUITACA DANCES

In the chair,
I dream again
of reaching
a hall of sweat
and Latin beats.

I am tense,
a pent-up hum,
a Colombian drum:
tambora,
tambor alegre, lamador;
I am seeds of *maracas*
and metal of *guaches.*

I am Huitaca,
rebel goddess
in full command
of the Moon:
my owl wings swell
with sensory pleasure.
I am bewitched
and bewitching.

I am Shakira
at the Superbowl,
a Hula-Hooping,
dance-trouping,
high-kicking,
wrist-curling
hair-flicking diva.
My Hips Don't Lie.

In the chair
that is my hall
of sweat and Latin beats,

I take this diagnosis, this disease,
this groundswell of grave-dark fears

and I dance them all to death: dance hard,
dance fierce, until they become tumbling dust

and nothing is left
but a drumbeat.

TRUST

I take my usual window-seat at my usual table.
I'm not a novelty here: no one shuns my gaze.

The café is an upmarket Italian chain offering;
the waitress told me her home town last time.
Afterwards, I might pop in to see if Space N.K.
has the eyeliner my oncologist recommended.

I'm pretty sure I have the best oncologist ever.
She knows how to mend my defective breast,

how to prevent tender eyes from gumming up,
how eye-shadow is like hot sand during chemo,
how the perfect eyebrow pencil is self-defence.

Yes, my oncologist is the best. She knows it all,
even that my shade is Moanda-Auburn-Warm.

ANGEL

The name Thembi carries meaning: *a gift, a promise, hope.*
Air is her element, Libra her sign. Her voice, thunder
deep, the rainy season swell of the lower Zambezi
flooding and greening her wasted homeland.

Thembi greeted me on the first day. I said nothing,
focused on staying alive. She held my hand lightly
and read out scriptures of side-effects; paused
as I took in the words that made me weep.

Thembi stood chairside while the red devil infused
commonplace poison. A warrior hardened by battle
with nausea, wrestling veins, she knew that nothing
and everything could be settled with tea and cake.

Thembi was my morning star, always switched on
a hundred watts bright, always so busy with need.
I never blamed her for my pain. Yes, she hurt me
sometimes – but always with a smile.

Thembi was there when my turn came to scatter
my hard-won peals of freedom into the air –
a celebration chime, the sound proclaimed:
I Am Done.

        And then   then she moved on,
waiting for the next lost soul, her book
of scripture at her side.

I think of Thembi on her rounds,
        her river laugh a rallying, ceaseless cry,
                flooding and filling, flooding and filling,

        and against all expectation, in my wasted soul
a soft greening begins.

A NOVICE IN WINTER

A watchful Mother Superior,
you welcome me day by day.

I'm a bride veiled in wintertime.
I might greet you today, or not.

In cloistered space, laser-cut dark,
I can choose the soundtrack

to the radiating darkness – and yet
I am cinched and clinched, metallic.

When I leave, it's with an embrace.
Your gaze is chiselled, chiding me –

"Progress!" – your expectant decree.
I can't live up to your example.

Maybe I could have done, before.
My bones have forgotten how.

CHERRYWOOD

First light: fingers reach for the box
that holds my pills, tactile, welcoming.
I chose this box, its cherrywood grain,
trees carved filigree in wan backlight,
an incarnation of the imprecise moon.

Someone crafted this box; put in time.
I see them working in the deep night
of unceasing winter, a big dog curled
at their feet, keeping close as if to say:
Stay here, inside. I'll keep you warm.

THE ANCIENT ART OF KINTSUGI

First, you must collect the fragments.
Proceed with care. They will be fragile.

Don't say it's not fair, don't ask why –
why it was your pot that smashed.
Focus on each shattered piece. Pray
that it will reveal its true shape, role,
destiny. Look for clues, pray again.

Tell your fragments to speak up, speak
louder than before. They are beautiful.
Say this often. Think it even when you
are somewhere else. They may begin
to hear this message and absorb it.

Though you may not believe it, this helps
cracks to heal until they are ghost-lines.
Belief will become glue that holds broken
parts together. Your words, given freely,
if you believe in them, are melted gold.

Next, mix your gold with *urushi* resin.
Coat the edges of each piece – be careful
not to apply it to skin. It's deadly if done
incorrectly. Place each shard, each fragment
next to another. Do they suggest a form?

Now, be prepared for your pot to tell you
that it has re-evaluated. That it is a pot
no longer. That it wants more for itself
and you: to be a lamp, a swan, a flute.
Maybe it only knows that it must hold –

hold together, hold on to itself, hold on
so as not to blow apart. Listen. Believe.

You should now be ready to try the pieces
and see if they fit. If so, great. If not, stick
together what you can. Fill any larger gaps
with more molten gold. This is *makienaoshi,*
a process developed for difficult cases.

Now, assess your pot, or lamp, or swan.
Hopefully, if you've followed each step
precisely and neglected none, you will find
your object transformed – imperfect still,
but almost resembling a whole.

HORMONE POSITIVE

The heat presses
my restless spine
until I would climb
of my own accord
into a bath of ice.
Swallowed whole,
a hormone cocktail
adds to the sweat
that dehydrates
and irrigates me.
Several times a day,
temperatures rise
to a hundred degrees.
A personal heatwave,
tessellating skin,
or the heat
presses me into
the swampy mattress.
Either way I am denied
respite. Inside
is outside, it's the same –
fierce sucking in oxygen
and I can bear
no more, yet
I must not
stop
taking it. I must be
patient. [1]

---

[1] The treatment plan for patients with hormone-positive breast cancer (also known as "ER+") may include five to ten years of hormone therapy. This reduces the risk of your own body using your estrogen to grow new cancer cells even more quickly. Hot flushes are one of the common side-effects of this therapy.

Eat ice cream to cool down
while I wait.
Or, I must not eat
ice cream at all.

Its richness
is the enemy, turns
my own fat cells
against me. I'll give
anything, do anything
to sizzle just one
snowflake
on my flat matt tongue.

HOW I HEAR IT

My dear, you cannot hope to be
well   again   without
putting in the hard yards

You are going to have to make
some effort   some changes
Let me see them
do I have to pry them
from between your fingers?

Just get out of bed   can't you
Just eat well   get your head   straight
You know I could cook   The kids and I want
something   different on our plate
It's okay   we can wait

Get some rest, now
Get up off the floor, now   the kids
the kids all the mess and all the things
Leave it all to me   where were you, asleep
again?

HINDSIGHT

All the pretty things

we acquired then
weigh insubstantial

against

the heaviness of what
we both gave up

MORTEN AND MARILYN

You're not to shave your legs, hear?
Mum calls upstairs as I laze away
in a bathtub of Body Shop bubbles.

Eyes closed, I'm imagining a world
where I could kiss away the tears
on Morten's chiselled cheekbones.

Who d'you think you are, young lady,
Marilyn Monroe? Remember, I told you
how she ended up?

We've rehearsed this a million times.
No, I flip back, casually cruel.
No, I don't, actually.

I know it. I know I could be the one.
I could kiss away his tears,
his exquisite pain.

I know I could. He doesn't need
to do a thing to help me.

MOTHERHOOD

Uppers and downers, she calls them on the phone.
I can't stop her mind racing like a hunted deer.
I need to explain, if I could just lift the brain-fog,
stop this conversation and start a different one.

How a quarter-tab, a friendly yellow flower,
sinks me into sleep. How I'm tired of trying
to negotiate prescriptions and insurance claims.
How I'm static, in stasis, stuck.

How my nights have become a PTSD perversion,
an unspooling loop of events in high definition.
How a slower tempo of days and nights and days
helps my face turn just a little towards the sun.

How I have seen her wearing a black dress for me,
as I have already worn a black dress for myself
and for my children as they walk alone to school.
How I have learned to let them find the way.

4.00 A.M. MANTRA

I didn't do this.
I didn't do this to myself.

I didn't do this to be in a special club.
I didn't do this to gain anyone's sympathy.
I didn't do this to have the perfect excuse to fail.

I didn't do this.
I didn't do this to myself.

I didn't do this to my husband.
I didn't do this to our small children.
I didn't do this to win love or shirk duty.

I didn't do this.
I didn't do this to myself.

I didn't do this to my parents, who expect to go first.
I didn't do this to my sisters, too young for these checks.
I didn't do this to my nieces, to my future granddaughters.

I didn't do this.
I didn't do this to myself.

(Repeat)

MUSCLE MEMORY

We drive to the reservoir and plant ourselves
by the waterfront. One by one the men dive,
scattering the water into bright crystal shards.

I am last to go, unwilling to show scars or rolls
of anti-depressant belly, my right arm swollen
with lymph fluid. My costume clings all wrong.

No one else quibbles, so in I plunge. Toes curl
in hope of a solid foundation, disappointed
by rocks that tumble sideways under pressure.

No choice but to swim, fixing my gaze on shore.
The sky is tranquil; good company for my travel,
only growing surly when the wind picks a fight.

On an outcrop, an elderly couple sit, leaning in,
relaxed, a picture of companionship. Amazing:
they must have hiked two kilometres round.

I want us to be like them; so poised, so balanced,
so natural. Hard as I try, my muscles cramping
with lactic acid, I find it impossible to push on.

CHEAT CODES – A FOUND POEM

I find a single sheet of A4 paper, printed on one side in
cheap ink.

Unlock All Arenas
Unlock All Bonus Stages

He must have done it at school, or maybe
a friend gave it to him in the playground.

Unlock All Concept Art

I like the idea of concept art. I do. Although: it's the kind of
thing we feel we should say we like, when in reality
we don't know what it is.

Unlock All Duel Characters

Sounds simple enough,
unless you've known any.

Unlock All Moves
Unlock All Powers and Moves
Now we're talking. Can I clarify –
are Moves / Powers and Moves mutually exclusive?
Can I have all of them? I'd like to have all of them.

Unlock All Story Levels
Unlock Super Light Sabre Mode
Unlock Tiny Droid Mode

Uh, Tiny Droid Mode?

Unlock Quick Health and Force Refill

    Yes

Unlock Infinite Health

             Yes

Unlock Infinite Force Power

                  Yes

UPHILL AT TRIFELS CASTLE [2]

Twenty minutes into the ascent,
the car park is a row of infant teeth.

When the skittering sky has stopped
galloping, I try to relocate my breath.
My lungs are shy of the steep incline.

Half-sunken stones are battle-scarred,
sundered and reconstructed, humming
with ancient blood debt, long repaid.

The consultant told me in brittle English
that his method would have been kinder,
conserving my traitorous lymph nodes.

But I was picked clean before we leapt
the short currents of the English Channel
and built our nest among the apple fields.

I was asleep and didn't get to say goodbye.
Now it's far too late to return, even if
I wanted to. Memory gives me nothing

to grasp. Scars fade. I was told that steel clips
were left behind, a signpost that should show up
at annual mammograms and, possibly, airports.

No one mentioned the steps, though. Look up.
Christ! They're waiting, hot and breathless.
The boys have run ahead, out of sight.

---

[2] Trifels is the hilltop castle in Germany where King Richard I of England,
The Lionheart, was held for ransom. Long a ruin, the castle was
reconstructed in the twentieth century in a new, Italianate design, nothing like
the original.

PETERSBERG [3]

These windows, thrown open,
show you these things:

A mountain, rocks, ruins, lowering clouds.
A river, blue, cool-glazed, mirroring trees.

A swallow is building a nest for its babies.
A little white ferry goes back and forth.

Shoulders soften, less like blades
than softly-feathered wings.

---

[3] Petersberg is one of the Siebengebirge ("Seven Mountains") Range that runs along the river Rhein near our home; a place of tranquility and peace with far-reaching views in all directions. I was fortunate enough to stay at the hotel at the summit for a self-care break.

ACKNOWLEDGEMENTS

Thank you to the brilliant Mark Davidson at Hedgehog Press for helping me to shine a light on the aftermath of breast cancer. My thanks also go to the editors of *Reach (Indigo Dreams)*, *Cheltenham Clean Air Project*, *Near Window*, *One Hand Clapping*, *Orchard Lea Press* and *Green Ink Poetry Press*, in whose publications various poems in this pamphlet first appeared.

I would like to thank Anna Saunders, Alison Powell and Jenny Robb for their support and guidance. Thank you to all my friends in the poetry community. You inspire me every day.

I am endlessly grateful to Mr Anup Sharma, Dr Muireann Kelleher, the staff of Cancer Centre London, Parkside Hospital, Macmillan and my local NHS GP Surgery for their unstinting support.

Heartfelt thanks to Agata Dlugosz for being our rock during my diagnosis, treatment and recovery. Thank you to the many wonderful friends and neighbours who supported and helped us. You held us close in our most difficult times.

Finally, all my love to my parents, Jan and Chris, my sisters, Juliet and Katy, my husband, Peter, and our sons, Gabriel and Raphael and my parents-in-law, Gabriele and Peter. Your support means the world to me.

ABOUT THE AUTHOR

Lucy Heuschen (she/her) is a British poet living in the countryside near Bonn, Germany with her family and rescue dog. Lucy is a former lawyer, breast cancer survivor, avid reader and anti-plastic blogger. She is the founder and editor of *The Rainbow Poems* and the *Sonnets for Shakespeare* anthology. She leads the German Stanza of the Poetry Society.

Lucy's poetry has been published in magazines and journals including *Reach, Sarasvati, Dawntreader, Beyond Words, Irisi, Covid Narratives, FEED, Unlimited, Near Window, The Great Margin, Poetry & Covid, One Hand Clapping* and *Green Ink*. She has contributed to anthologies by Black Bough, Dreich, New Contexts, Yaffle and Hedgehog Press.

You can connect with Lucy on Twitter @Rainbow_Poems, on Facebook @RainbowPoemsUK and via her website, www.therainbowpoems.co.uk.